Children's Edition

Stop Reading, Start Studying:
Searching for God's Hidden Treasure

Henry Jackson III

Ordering Information:

Quantity sales. Special discounts are available on quantity purchases by non-profits, ministries, churches, corporations, associations, and others. For details, contact the publisher via email at sales@inductivebiblestudyapp.com.

Printed in the United States of America
First Printing, 2016

ISBN

Paperback: 978-0-9970743-8-3
Kindle: 978-0-9970743-9-0

www.InductiveBibleStudyApp.com

Because of the dynamic nature of the internet, any web addresses or links contained in this book may have changed since publication and may no longer be valid.

Inductive Bible Study
Stop reading, start studying!

At Inductive Bible Study LLC, our mission is simple – "make disciples of all nations" (Matt. 28:19). We are committed to providing high quality tools, resources, and training to assist Christ's church in fulfilling the Great Commission.

Thank you for purchasing or downloading one of our resources!

Also available:

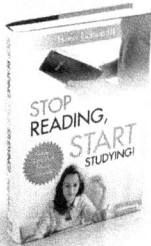

Book

The premier book on how to enrich your study of God's word using the Inductive Bible Study method!

Paperback: 978-0- 9970743-0- 7

Kindle: 978-0- 9970743-1- 4

ePub: 978-0- 9970743-2- 1

Audiobook: 978-0- 9970743-3- 8

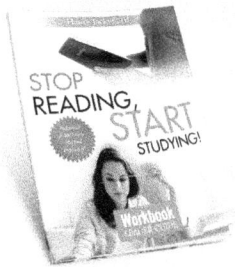

Student Workbook

This five lesson study provides practical steps on how to study the Bible inductively, memorize & meditate on Scripture, and pray effectively.

Paperback: 978-0- 9970743-5- 2

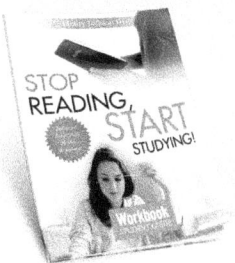

Leader Guide

This guide empowers small group leaders with discussion starters, background commentary and easy to follow lesson plans.

Paperback: 978-0- 9970743-4- 5

Kindle: 978-0- 9970743-6- 9

If this resource has helped you enhance in your walk with God, please help spread the word about us.

Facebook: /InductiveBibleStudyApp

Twitter: @iBibleStudyApp

Google+: InductiveBibleStudyApp

Email: info@ibible.study

YouTube: InductiveBibleStudyApp

Web: http://ibible.study

Check out our free IBS app - http://InductiveBibleStudyApp.com

Table of Contents

Introduction

Welcome to Inductive Bible Study! It's never too early to begin teaching children to study God's Word!

The Bible says we should diligently teach God's Word to children:

"And these words that I command you today shall be on your heart. You shall teach them diligently to your children, and shall talk of them when you sit in your house, and when you walk by the way, and when you lie down, and when you rise." (Deut. 6:6-7 ESV)

This Children's Edition of Stop Reading, Start Studying: Searching for God's Hidden Treasure! provides five easy-to-follow lessons centered on the idea that searching for "deep and hidden things" (Dan. 2:22) in the Bible is like going on an exciting treasure hunt! Even children who have never opened a Bible before will come away eager to study God's Word!

Each lesson will teach children how to explore the hidden treasures of the Bible. The first three lessons of the book will walk kids through the fundamental steps to Inductive Bible Study (observation, interpretation and application) using kid-friendly language. Then, Lesson 4 will talk about the importance of memorizing and meditating on Scripture. Lesson 5 will help kids understand what prayer is and why it is an essential step to Bible study. Each lesson includes a focus Scripture, the main point, a suggested song with lyrics, and a biblical lesson in story form—written in a way that is easy for kids to understand. The story follows with a related circle time activity called "Why It Matters," and finally a fun craft that ties the whole lesson together.

By helping children to understand a few simple steps and the "how" of Inductive Bible Study, leaders will spur kids toward an intimate relationship with God at a young age. Children will begin to learn how to interpret God's Word accurately and apply it to their lives, thereby experiencing its life-transforming power!

An overview of the Inductive Bible Study app is provided in the appendix followed by a copy of the helpful charts presented in the workbook. Feel free to make as many copies of the charts as you'd like.

This Children's Edition of Stop Reading, Start Studying! Searching for God's Hidden Treasure! serves as an excellent companion to the associated adult book (Stop Reading, Start Studying: Inductive Bible Study Method Explained). However, it functions independently as it has been adapted for leaders to use as a tool to instruct children ages 1st through 5th grade in how to study the Bible inductively.

The lessons are perfect for weekly Sunday School, a week-long VBS, or in conjunction with a church-wide course on how to study God's Word. Each lesson lends itself to the flexibility of being completed in one setting or it can be broken up into multiple sessions.

Inductive Bible Study is not hard! But it does take time. The techniques laid out in the Stop Reading, Start Studying: Searching for God's Hidden Treasure! will change the way kids read, study and interpret the Bible, and ultimately, it will change their life.

LESSON 1

DIGGING FOR GOLD

Observation:
Pay Attention to Each Word!

Key Verse

"All Scripture is inspired by God and is useful for teaching and for showing people what is wrong in their lives." - 2 Timothy 3:16

Main Point

Every word in the Bible is important. "Observation" means looking at each word of the Bible like you are going on a treasure hunt to find out what God is saying . . . it's like finding gold!

Song

The Bible is the Treasure!

The Bible is the treasure
I open it and I see
Jesus wants to be my friend
And God loves me

The Bible is the treasure
I read it and I find
I'm part of God's big family
And He loves me all the time...All the time!

Yo ho ho, Yo ho ho! Yo ho ho—the Bible is the treasure!

Yo ho ho, Yo ho ho! Yo ho ho—the Bible is the treasure!

A link to a video of the above song is available at http://ibible.study/children.

Story Time

"Jesus and the Great Storm" - *Mark 4:35–41*

Jesus was a great teacher. He taught all kinds of stories to help people understand God and heaven. When Jesus spoke, everybody listened to every word!

One day, Jesus had been teaching thousands and thousands of people all day in the sun, near the Sea of Galilee. It is actually a great big lake. After a long day of teaching, he said to His twelve followers, "Let's all get in that boat, and sail to the other side of the lake! We are all so tired, and we need a break from all of these people."

> **Question:** Where had Jesus been teaching people all day?
> **Answer:** Near the Sea of Galilee

Now many of Jesus' followers had jobs as fisherman. This means they were professional fishermen! Back then, they used boats that were made out of cedar wood, and had a flat bottom. They would throw nets over the side of the boat to catch their fish—and they did this every day! They were experts on the water! They knew how to steer a boat and to be in charge of rough water because they had been in many storms before.

But this time, they were frightened. It was a terrible storm. And on top of that, Jesus had fallen asleep! One of Jesus' disciples said, "Should we wake Him up?" and another said, "How can he sleep when the waves are so big and the wind is so fierce?"

They tried everything they could to steer the boat to the shore and save their lives. But nothing worked. They didn't want to bother their Master, but there was nothing they could do and the boat was about to sink. They were terrified, thinking they were going to die!

Finally they shook Him awake. "Teacher! Teacher!" they cried. "Don't you care if we drown?"

> **Question:** What job did many of the disciples have?
> **Answer:** They were fishermen.

Jesus sat up, rubbed His eyes, and looked around. Indeed there was a violent storm. He stood up and actually talked to the waves like they were people! "Quiet!" he said in a loud voice. "Be still!" Instantly the winds stopped. The waves calmed and the water turned flat once again. The only thing the disciples heard was the sound of water softly lapping up against the side of the boat.

"Where is your faith?" Jesus said. "Why are you afraid?"

The followers must have looked at each other with wide eyes. They must have been shaking their heads in disbelief!

Even the wind and the water listened to Jesus' words!

Why It Matters

- Is anyone afraid of bad storms?

- Is anyone scared of thunder and lightning?

- How do you feel during a bad storm?

Just imagine being on a boat during a storm and how scary that would be! Think of the big waves tossing the boat this way and that, and the water spraying all over your face.

Let's look at some of the details of this story. I'm going to read it to you straight from the Bible and I want you to listen very carefully, okay?

That evening, Jesus said to his followers, "Come with me across the lake." He and the followers left the people there. They went in the boat that Jesus was already sitting in. There were also other boats with them. A very strong wind came up on the lake. The waves began coming over the sides and into the boat. It was almost full of water. Jesus was at the back of the boat, sleeping with his head on a pillow. The followers went to Him and woke Him. They said, "Teacher, do you care about us? We will drown!" Jesus stood up and commanded the wind and the waves to stop. He said, "Quiet! Be still!" Then the wind stopped, and the lake became calm. Jesus said to his followers, "Why are you afraid? Do you still have no faith?"

The followers were very afraid and asked each other, "What kind of man is this? Even the wind and the waves obey Him!"

- Matthew 4:35–41

We can learn a lot from this story just by looking at the details. This is called "OBSERVATION."

Let's see if we can figure out some of the details that give us more understanding of what God is trying teach us!

- Who is Jesus with?

- Where are Jesus and His followers? (At the Sea of Galilee/the lake)

- What is the weather like?

- Why were Jesus' followers so scared?

- How did Jesus stop the bad storm?

See how much you learned about the story? Every word in the Bible is important!

Craft: Telescope

Materials

- Colored paper cup

- Toilet paper roll/Paper towel roll

- Colored paper to match the colored paper cup, cut in a rectangle the size of the toilet paper/paper towel roll

- Glue or tape

- Colored markers

- Scissors

- Pirate Stickers or Self-Adhesive Jewels

Instructions

Younger Children:

Have younger children tape the colored paper around the toilet paper roll. Use markers and pirate stickers to decorate the "telescope."

Older Children:

Wrap the paper towel roll with colored paper that matches the paper cup. Place the paper towel roll on the bottom of the cup and trace around the roll. Cut out that circle so the roll can fit through the cup. Once the roll is inserted into the cup, have an adult use a glue gun to glue the paper cup to the paper towel roll (a few beads of glue will do the trick). Decorate the telescope with pirate stickers, self-adhesive jewels, or markers!

Finished Product

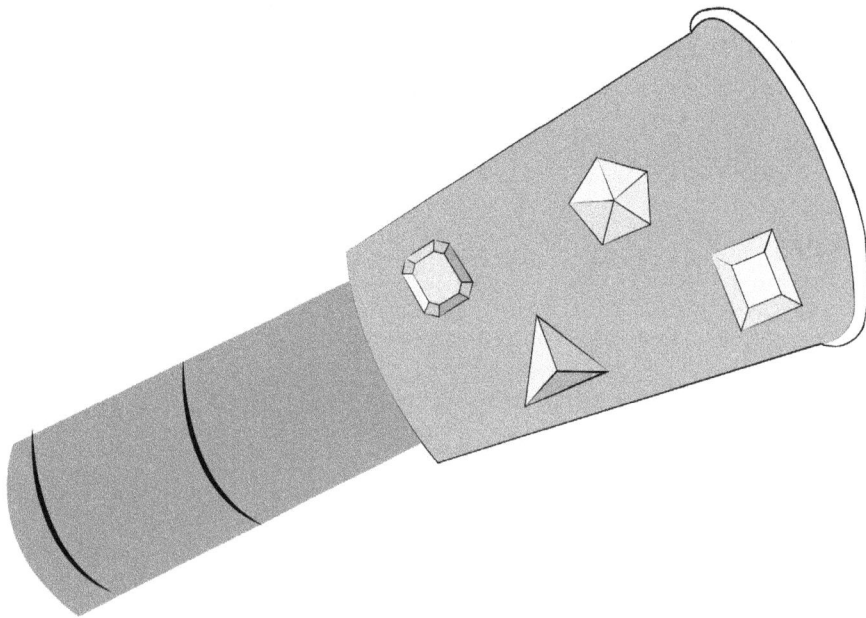

```
Craft Time Topic
```

Talk about what a real telescope does—how it makes objects that are far away look closer. Talk about how observing stories in the Bible is like using a telescope—seeing things that might be hard to see at first.

LESSON 2
HIDDEN TREASURE

Interpretation:
Searching for God's Treasure

Key Verse

"Be a worker who is not ashamed of his work—a worker who uses the true teaching in the right way." - 2 Timothy 2:15b

Main Point

Each passage of the Bible has meaning, and "interpreting" the Bible means trying to figure out what that meaning is. It is like hunting for a hidden treasure!

Song

The B-I-B-L-E

The B-I-B-L-E
Yes, that's the book for me
I stand alone on the Word of God
The B-I-B-L-E

The B-L-O-O-D
That Jesus shed for me
Christ paid the price,
Our sacrifice
The B-L-O-O-D!

I'm S-A-V-E-D,
By G-R-A-C-E;
I'm saved by grace,
The Scripture says
The B-I-B-L-E

A link to a video of the above song is available at http://ibible.study/children.

Story Time

"Jesus on the Road to Emmaus" - *Luke 24:13–35*

Jesus, who is the best teacher in the world and the Savior for every person who believes in Him, had died on the cross and was buried. Two of Jesus' followers were leaving Jerusalem after it happened. They were walking on a long, dusty road in sandals and long robes to a town called Emmaus—it was a seven-mile trip! Their feet were dirty. They were probably thirsty. And they were very, very sad.

Just then, a man appeared out of nowhere! He started walking with the two men and noticed their sadness. "What are you discussing together as you walk along?" he asked.

"How come you don't know what happened today!" one of the men said. "Everybody in Israel knows!" But the strange man said he didn't know! "What things?" the man said. "Tell me!"

> **Question:** Who was walking on the road to Emmaus?
> **Answer:** Two of Jesus' followers.

So Jesus' followers told the strange man everything that had just happened. On three days ago, Jesus, who we thought God sent to help us, was crucified—he was hung on a cross to die. Then He was buried in a tomb, and a huge, heavy stone was rolled in front of the tomb with a soldier to guard it so no one would take his body. On today, we heard some shocking news! Some women went to the tomb early this morning and met an angel who told them that Jesus is alive – he rose from the dead!

Suddenly, the strange man who had been walking with them said, "Don't you remember what the prophets from long ago said about this? The prophets said the Savior would have to go through terrible things—even die!" Then the strange man taught Jesus' two followers everything the Bible said about the Savior.

Question: What did the strange man tell Jesus' followers that the Bible is about?
Answer: The Savior.

The three men finally arrived in Emmaus, tired and very hungry! They sat down to eat dinner, and just then, when the strange man tore a piece of bread to eat, the two men realized . . . it was Jesus! He was sitting right there at the table with them! They couldn't believe what their eyes were seeing! They looked at each other and probably thought, "How can this be?"

Immediately, Jesus disappeared! Just like that! (Snap fingers). The two men said to each other, "Our hearts were bouncing around in our chest when Jesus was walking with us on the dusty road! He was telling us what the Bible said about the Savior! Everything is true! Jesus is the Savior, and He is alive!"

Why It Matters

Question: What is a treasure?
Answer: Something valuable—gold, jewels, gems, something important.

Question: Why would you want to find a treasure?
Answer: It could be worth a lot of money!

Hide a dollar bill somewhere in the class!

Explain to the children you have hidden a dollar bill somewhere in the classroom. You are going to give the 30 seconds to try and find it!

Regroup after the children search for the dollar bill.

This is how the Bible is! Only at the right time and the right place, God is the one who helps us to see what the "prize" or the "treasure" is that is hidden. (Now, show them where you hid the dollar bill if it hasn't been found.) The whole Bible is full of those treasures, and we have to go on a treasure hunt to find them!

When Jesus was walking with the two men to Emmaus, He was talking to them about Himself. But how? He used the Bible! He went to the parts of the Bible that are very old—like thousands of years old. But those parts of the Bible talked about Jesus and gave clues to people about Jesus. Searching for these clues to help us understand what we are reading is called "INTERPRETATION." Can you say that with me? Interpretation. Interpretation means to find out what something in the Bible means.

Jesus helped the two men understand why Jesus died and was buried. He also helped them understand that God said He would come back to life again!

The Bible will tell us everything we need to know about Jesus—and about other things in the Bible, too.

Craft: Treasure Hunt Craft

Materials

- Light brown construction paper copied with "Treasure Map"

- Treasure Map Clues

- Treasure Map Cutouts

- Self-Adhesive Jewels

- Treasure hunt stickers

- Glue sticks

- Twine

Instructions

Younger Children:

Give kids the photocopied treasure map and a set of the cut out symbols that correspond with the clues. Read the clue, and when someone answers in the group (or all) let the kids glue the image of the "clue" on the map in the corresponding circle. Let them use the remaining time to decorate their map with jewels and other treasure hunt stickers. * *You may have to give the answers to younger kids.*

The treasure at the end of the clues is Jesus! Glue the Jesus picture on the "X."

Talk with the kids while they are working on their map of all things that might be obstacles to searching for the treasure. When finished, roll the map up and tie the map with a piece of twine!

Older Children:

Have children scrunch the brown paper in a ball and then unroll it, so it has an old, "treasure map" look. Give the kids a photocopy of the Scripture "clues" and let them come up with the answers, working with each other. Ask "Who is the answer to all of these clues?" Jesus! He is the ultimate treasure. Have them glue the Jesus picture on the "X."

Craft Time Topic

Talk with the kids while they are working on their map about things that might be obstacles to searching for the treasure—or even why it might be hard to figure out what something in the Bible means. Talk about how ancient Bible times were very different then today—the culture was different and sometimes it helps to understand the culture when we try to find out what a passage means.

When finished, roll the map up and tie the map with a piece of twine!

Finished Product

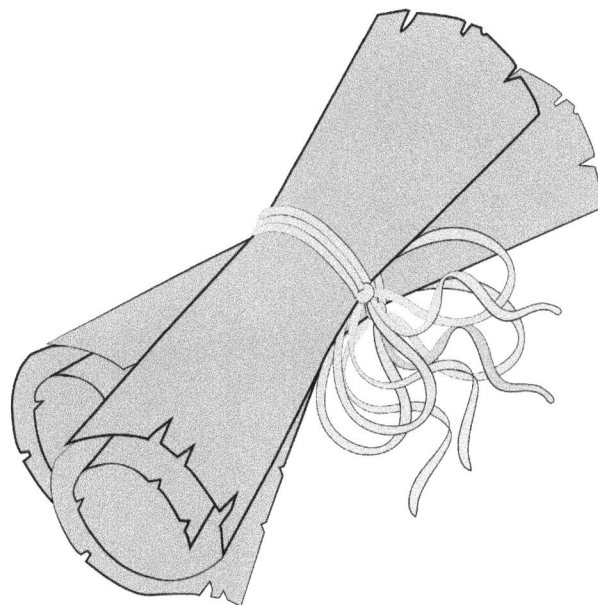

Clue 1

Clue 2

Clue 3

Clue 4

Clue 5

Treasure Map Clues

CLUE 1: "I will give you the _____ of the kingdom of heaven."
– Matthew 16:19

CLUE 2: "To him who knocks, the _____ will be opened."
– Matthew 7:8

CLUE 3: "Trust in the Lord with all your_____"
– Proverbs 3:5

CLUE 4: Your word is a _____ to my feet and a light for my path.
– Psalm 119:105

CLUE 5: "For the word of God is alive and active. Sharper than any double-edged _____, it penetrates even to dividing soul and spirit, joints and marrow; it judges the thoughts and attitudes of the heart.

Treasure Map Clues

CLUE 1: "I will give you the _____ of the kingdom of heaven." – Matthew 16:19

Answer: KEYS

CLUE 2: "To him who knocks, the _____ will be opened." – Matthew 7:8

Answer: DOOR

CLUE 3: "Trust in the Lord with all your_____" – Proverbs 3:5

Answer: HEART

CLUE 4: Your word is a _____ to my feet and a light for my path. – Psalm 119:105

Answer: LAMP

CLUE 5: "For the word of God is alive and active. Sharper than any double-edged _____, it penetrates even to dividing soul and spirit, joints and marrow; it judges the thoughts and attitudes of the heart.

Answer: SWORD

Treasure Map Cutouts

LESSON 3

CASHING IN

Application:
What Do I Do With the Treasure?

Key Verse

"Loving God means obeying his commands. And God's commands are not too hard for us." - 1 John 5:3

Main Point

Application is reading God's Word, and doing what it says. It is choosing to believe the treasure you have just discovered!

Song

I Have Decided to Follow Jesus

I have decided to follow Jesus
I have decided to follow Jesus
I have decided to follow Jesus
No turning back, no turning back

Tho' none go with me, I still will follow
Tho' none go with me I still will follow
Tho' none go with me, I still will follow
No turning back, no turning back

My cross I'll carry, till I see Jesus
My cross I'll carry till I see Jesus
My cross I'll carry till I see Jesus
No turning back, No turning back

The world behind me, the cross before me
The world behind me, the cross before me
The world behind me, the cross before me
No turning back, no turning back

* A link to a video of the above song is available at http://ibible.study/children.

Story Time

"Go And Leave Your Country!" - *Genesis 12:1-7*

Abram was a man who lived a long time ago in a city called Haran. His wife was Sarai, and Abram and Sarai had no children. They were very sad about this, because they wanted children of their own.

Then, God appeared to Abram, and He spoke to him! Abraham must have been very, very afraid.

> **Question:** What was Abram's wife's name?
> **Answer:** Sarai

God told Abram to pack up everything he owned—all his camels, his tents, and his clothing—and leave Haran!

Then God told Abram something amazing. He told Abram that one day he would have so many children that they would grow into an entire nation! These many children are called "descendants." And there would be millions and millions of them! God said these descendants would one day bless everyone on the whole earth.

But there was a problem!

> **Question:** What do you think the problem was?
> **Answer:** Abram didn't have any children!

I wonder if Abram thought he was hearing strange voices in his head! Or maybe he thought God was crazy. How could Abram have millions of descendants, if he couldn't even have one baby?

But here is the amazing thing! The Bible says three words about how Abram responded to God's command to leave Haran and go to a different and new land—one that God would later show him. Do you know what those words were?

"So Abram went."

Even though it sounded like God was not making any sense, Abram obeyed God. The Bible says he packed up everything he owned "just as the Lord told him," and set out for a new land called Canaan. He took his nephew, Lot, and his wife, Sarai, with him. He was an old man when he left Haran—75 years old!

Why It Matters

- What are some things your mom and dad ask you to do that you don't like doing? (Hopeful responses: making your bed, emptying the dishwasher, being nice to a sibling, etc.)

Imagine how Abraham must have felt when God told him to pack up and go to a whole different country! Back then they didn't have moving trucks or airplanes. They had camels! It wasn't easy to move to a different country, because you had to walk there!

- If God asked you to pack your suitcase and move to a different school or city tomorrow, how would you respond?

But Abram followed God's instructions, even when it was hard. And God rewarded Abram for obeying – He *did* make him into a great nation!

Anybody can read the Bible. Anybody can study the Bible. But God asks us to obey what the Bible says! This is called "APPLICATION." Application means obeying what God teaches you in the Bible!

When we obey God's Word, some wonderful things happen! You have happier relationships with your family and your friends. Other people will see God's light shining on us.

- Do you know the best way we can show that we love God? (Solicit responses)

The best way we can show God we love Him is by obeying His instructions, just like Abram did—even when they sometimes don't make sense. This is like finding a big piece of gold or another treasure in the river, and taking it to the bank and getting money for it, instead of digging a big hole in the sand and burying the treasure forever!

- Can you think of some ways that you can obey what God tells us in the Bible?

(Hopeful responses: Being kind to others, obeying your parents, praying every day, believing in Jesus, etc).

Craft: Walking Stick

Abram Obeys and Goes to a New Land

Materials

- Washi tape in many different colors, or paint & brushes

- ¾" X 48" wooden dowels, or actual sticks are better!

- Beads

- String cut in 6" pieces

- Feathers

- Hot glue

This is a no-mess craft if you use the Washi tape! But, establish rules prior to beginning the craft that these are not to be used as weapons! Anyone who does will not be able to participate in the craft.

Explain that these are walking sticks like Abram may have used when leaving Haran for the new country! The walking sticks represent obeying God's Word. Just like Abram obeyed God when he received God's "treasure," so we must too. When we find a treasure when studying God's Word, even if it is something we need to do or change, we should obey like Abram.

Instructions

Younger Children:

After explaining the "rules," give children the dowels/sticks and tape and let them go to town! Or, use paint to create rings around the dowels/sticks.

Older Children:

After decorating the walking stick, tie a feather to the end of one piece of string. Add a bead and secure the feathers inside the bead. Add more beads. Tie the string to the top of the stick with a simple knot (will work best if the string is tied around the dowel at the top of where tape has already been wrapped around, so the string doesn't slide down). A tiny bead of hot glue will help this.

Finished Product

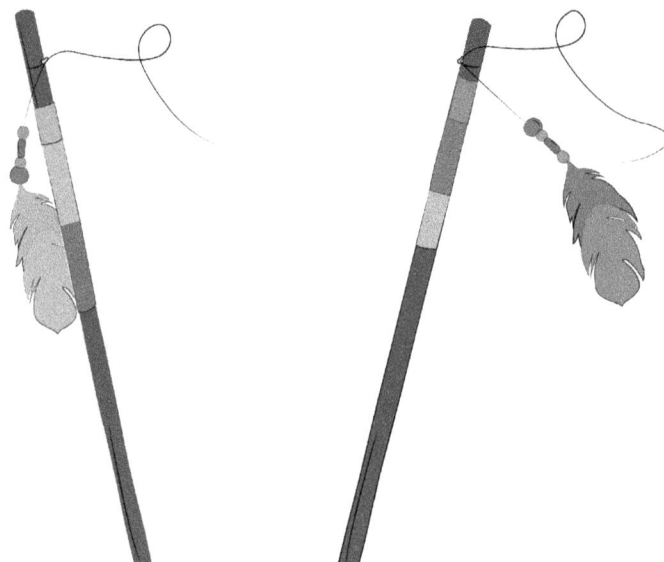

LESSON 4

SAVING FOR LATER

Memorization and Meditation:
Treasure God's Word

Key Verse

"Your word I have treasured in my heart, That I may not sin against You."
- Psalm 119:11 NASB

Main Point

God's word is a guide. It helps us do the things that please Him. That is why it is important to "memorize" verses, so they will always be available when we need God's Word to guide us. Encourage children to memorize the week's main memory before they come back the next day.

Song

The Psalm 119 Song

I have hidden your word in my heart – In my heart!
That I might not sin against you – Wahoo!
Psalm 119 verse 11
I have hidden your Word in my heart!

 * A link to a video of the above song is available at http://ibible.study/children.

"Jesus Tempted in the Wilderness" - *Matthew 4:1–11*

Jesus had just been baptized! It was a beautiful day at the Jordan River, but after Jesus came out of the water He had to face a big challenge. Today we will take an unusual journey! We will follow Jesus into the wilderness where no people live—only wild beasts and plants.

"I wonder what is going to happen?" Jesus may have thought. He had just been baptized a few days before in a river! It was a wonderful experience—God's voice was even heard from heaven saying, "I am very proud of my Son!" But now, Jesus was in a desert all by Himself.

Jesus ate nothing for 40 days and nights. He must have been very, very hungry and very thirsty! Just then, who shows up? The devil! The devil is always against God and Jesus. He wanted to try to tempt Jesus in to doing something that would make God sad.

The very first thing he said to Jesus was, "If you are so great, why don't you turn these rocks into bread? Then you won't be hungry in this wilderness anymore! Now Jesus could have asked God to turn rocks into bread and it would have happened like that! (Snap fingers). But is that what Jesus said to the devil? No!

He said, "It is written in the Scriptures, 'A person does not live only by eating bread. But a person lives by everything the Lord says.'"

Question: What did the devil try and get Jesus to do?
Answer: Turn rocks into bread

The devil was not happy. He was trying very hard to get Jesus to make a mistake, and not trust God. He wanted Jesus to believe him, instead of God! So he took Jesus to a beautiful city, the city of Jerusalem. He took Jesus to the Temple. The devil said, "If you really are God's Son, you should be able to do anything! If you jump off a high place, God will save you before you hit the ground. Your body won't even touch one rock!" The devil smiled . . . this time Jesus will show off His power, he thought!

Jesus calmly answered the devil, saying, "It also says in the Scriptures, 'Do not test the Lord your God.'"

Now, the devil was *really* mad.

Question: What did the devil try and get Jesus to do this time?
Answer: Jump off a high rock and save Himself!

The devil growled. He paced back and forth and tapped his chin with his pointer finger, deep in thought. How can I tempt Jesus now?" he thought. "Aha! I will take Jesus to the top of a very high mountain," he thought. "Look at all of these beautiful kingdoms! You could have all of this and be the most powerful man in the whole world!" Surely Jesus would believe this and turn away from God!

So the devil led Jesus to the top of a very high mountain. He stretched his hand out and showed Jesus all the kingdoms of the world and all the great things that are in those kingdoms. The devil said, "If you will bow down and treat me like the only king in the world, I will give you all of these powerful kingdoms! You will have the most power of anyone in the world!"

What an offer! But Jesus did not budge. He said firmly, "Go away from me, Satan! It is written in the Scriptures, 'You must worship the Lord your God. Serve only him!'"

Finally, the devil left Jesus. "I am so exhausted from being tempted," Jesus thought to Himself, pondering everything that had just happened. God sent some angels to come to Jesus to take care of Him.

Question: What did the devil try and get Jesus to do this third time?

Answer: Worship him!

Why It Matters

> - Has anyone ever been camping? Tell me what it's like?

When I think of camping I think of sleeping bags, bonfires, and beautiful stars in a dark sky.

> - What do you think of? What one thing do you make sure to bring?

Jesus spent a long time in the wilderness once, a full 40 days! That is a long camping trip—especially without food! What do you think He brought with Him on this trip?

Do you know what He brought? Only one thing! He didn't bring marshmallows or a sleeping bag or a tent.

He brought God's Word—but it wasn't even a Bible like you and I have. He brought God's Word in His heart!

The Bible tells us that when the devil tempted Jesus in the wilderness, Jesus responded by saying, "It says in the Scriptures..." How did Jesus know what the Bible said? He didn't have a Bible with Him in the wilderness!

He had Bible verses hidden, or "treasured" in His heart. This means He had those verses memorized and when the devil was trying to get Him to make a wrong choice, Jesus used God's Word to know what to do!

It's important to memorize verses, so they will always be available when we need their guidance, too.

- Have you ever memorized anything? Think of a song that you can sing by heart. That's what we should do with the Bible!

Craft: Treasure Box Craft - Hide God's Word in Heart

Materials

- Treasure Box Template A or B – Photocopied on brown paper

- Bible cut out (attached) or small Bible sticker

- Jewels

- Glue

- Tape

- Bible verses printed on light brown paper

Instructions

Younger Children:

Have Template "A" copied and pre-cut for younger children. Fold the top of the treasure box down. On the inside of the flap, have children glue jewels and a photocopied Bible image or a Bible sticker. Talk about the Word of God being a treasure "hidden in our heart" as kids work on their craft.

Older Children

Have older children cut out the copy of the treasure box, Template "B." Fold at the seams, and tape the treasure box together—leaving the top hinged to open and close. Give kids the photocopied list of Scriptures that they can cut into strips and put into the treasure chest, to begin to memorize at home. Talk about the Word of God being a treasure "hidden in our heart" as kids work on their craft.

Finished Product

Based on Template A:

Based on Template B

Treasure Box

Template A

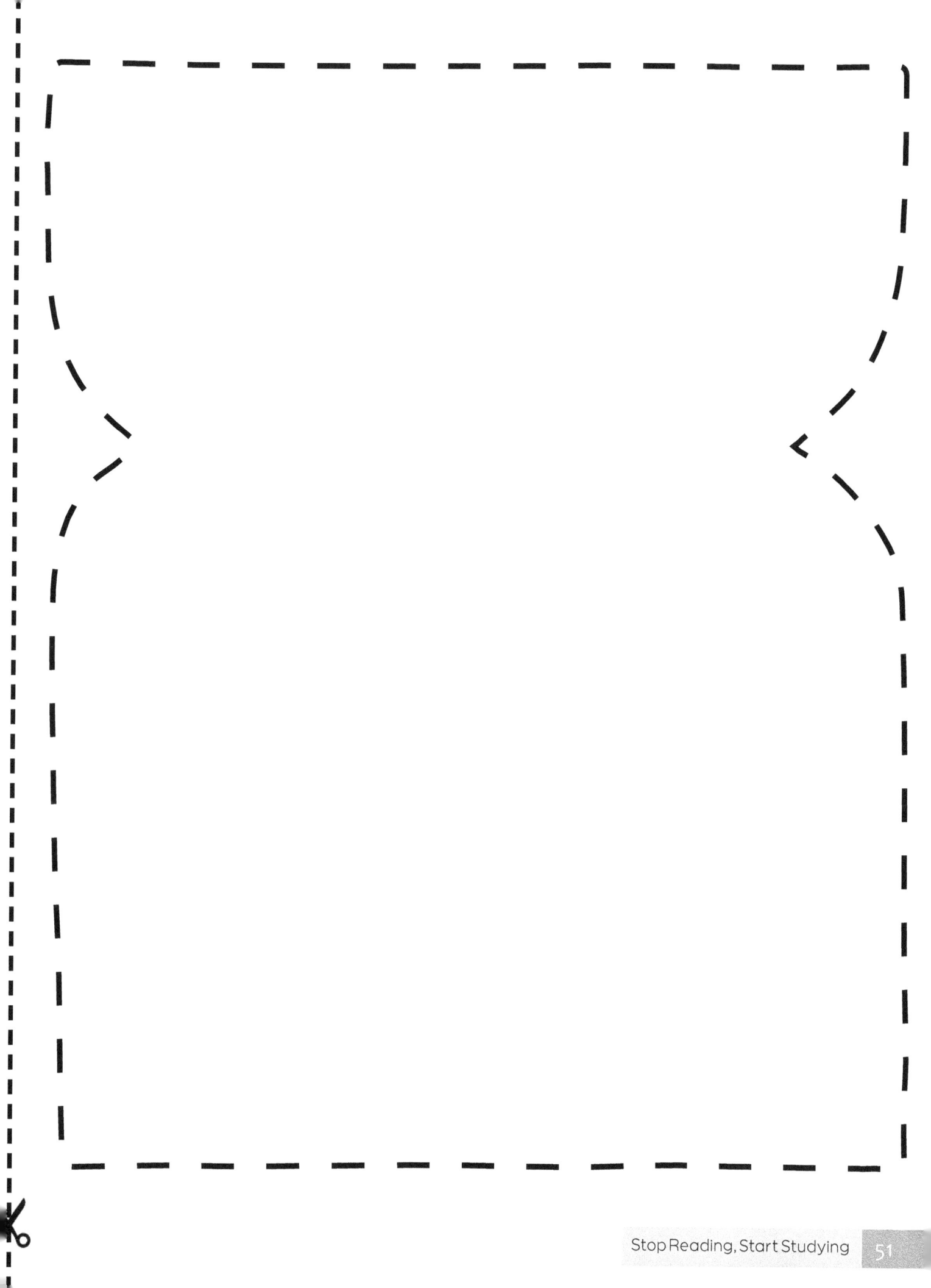

Treasure Box
Template B

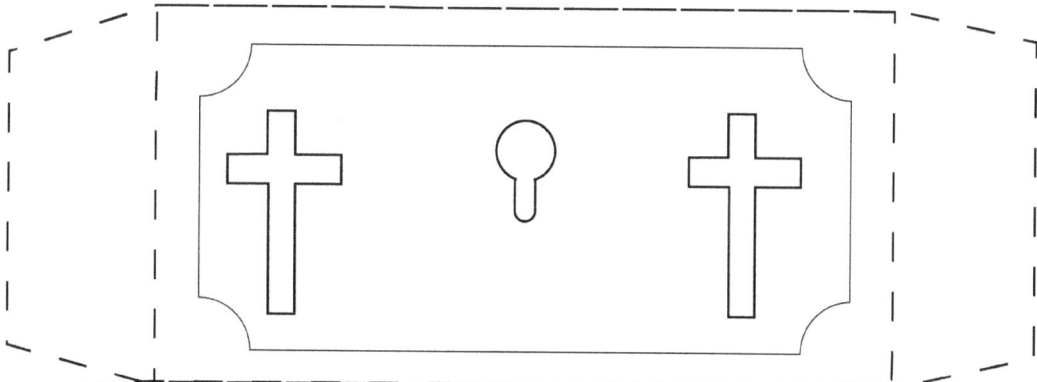

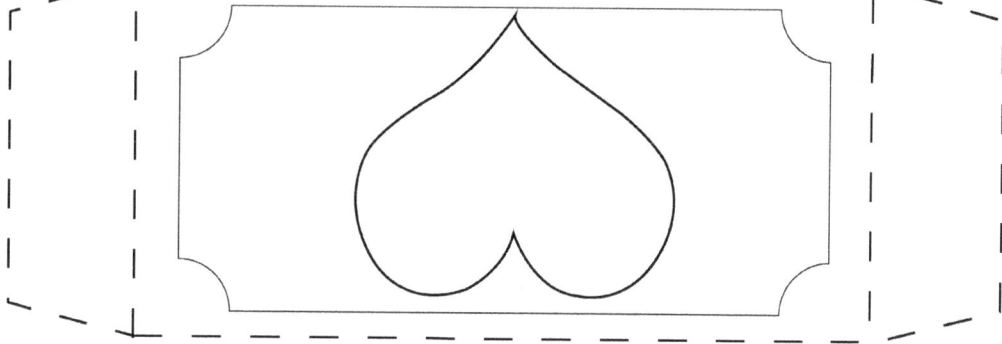

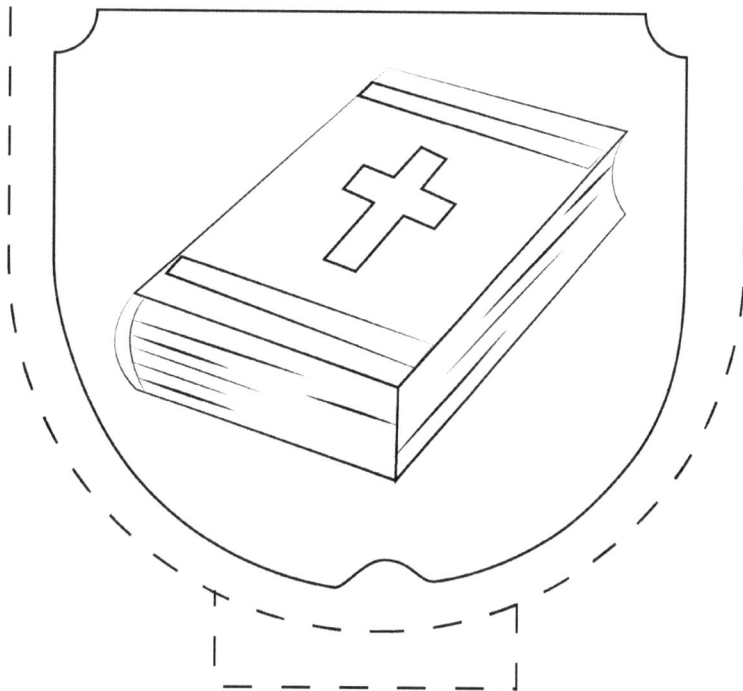

Treasure Box "Template B" Scriptures

Acts 16:31 – Believe on the Lord Jesus Christ, and you will be saved

Psalm 145:9 -The LORD is good to all.

Genesis 16:13 – You are the God who sees.

Proverbs 3:5 – Trust in the Lord with all your heart.

Proverbs 14:5 – An honest witness does not lie, a false witness breaths lies

Colossians 3:2 – Set your minds on things above, not on earthly things.

Colossians 3:16 – Let the word of Christ dwell in you richly

1 John 5:3 – This is love for God: to obey his commands

Ephesians 4:30 – And do not grieve the Holy Spirit

LESSON 5
TALK TO THE OWNER

Prayer:
Giving Treasures Back to God

Key Verse

"And pray in the Spirit on all occasions with all kinds of prayers and requests."
– Ephesians 6:18, NIV

Main Point

Through the Bible, God speaks to us. In prayer, we speak to God.

Song

Whisper a Prayer

Whisper a prayer in the morning
Whisper a prayer at noon
Whisper a prayer in the ev'ning
To keep your heart in tune

God answers prayer in the morning
God answers prayer at noon
God answers prayer in the ev'ning
To keep your heart in tune

Jesus may come in the morning
Jesus may come at noon
Jesus may come in the ev'ning

So keep your heart in tune

* A link to a video of the above song is available at
http://ibible.study/children.

Story Time

"The Persistent Widow" - *Luke 18:1–8*

Jesus told many stories to help people understand what He was trying to teach them. These stories are called "parables." Jesus told parables all the time because they helped people in Bible times understand some of the hard things He was teaching.

> **Question:** What is a "parable"?
> **Answer:** A story to help people understand something that is hard to understand.

One time Jesus taught a parable to help His followers to understand a little bit more about prayer—and that they should never give up when praying!

The story went like this: Once in a certain town there was a judge who did not follow God, and he didn't care one bit about what people thought about him. A poor, old widow kept making the long trip on dusty roads to see judge. A widow is someone whose husband has died—so this woman was all alone. Now judges are supposed to be fair and even-Steven, with all people. Apparently there was a person who was giving her a hard time, almost like an enemy. So the widow asked the judge to rule against this enemy! She asked the judge over and over, "Please grant justice against this unfair person!"

But the judge refused and refused.

But the judge began to think about it. He tapped his pointer finger on his chin and said, "Hmmm. Even though I don't believe in God and I don't care what people think about me, I'm going to answer this widow because she won't stop bothering me!

Question: Why did the judge finally answer the widow?

Answer: Because she didn't stop asking for his help!

Why It Matters

Materials

- Clothesline

- Clothespins

- index cards

- markers (for the older kids)

Instructions

Hold out a clothesline so the kids can see—a white rope with clothes pins attached. It should be long enough to go from one child and loop back to the teacher.

> **Question:** Do you know what this is? Do you know what it is used for?
> **Answer:** A clothesline.

Explain how clotheslines work, especially in bigger cities where you can pull clothes in from drying outside, because they are on a pulley. Tell kids when we talk to God we can imagine we have a line directly to Him!

Have one child the middle of the clothesline, while you hold both ends, and tell the child to close his or her eyes. Hold the other end yourself. Hold the line tight.

- **Ask the child:** Can you feel that I am on the end—even with your eyes closed?

This is like God! God is alive and active even though you can't see Him! But He is moving in your life!

Now, tell the student open his/her eyes, and shake the rope. Now close _your_ eyes.

- **Say:** Now I can feel you! When we pray, it's like we shake God's rope. There isn't a prayer that He doesn't hear, see or feel!

Question: If you really, really wanted something from God, how hard would you shake the rope?"
(Let the student shake the rope really hard).
How long would you shake the rope?
Answer: Until God answered!

If we really want something from God, we have to be persistent, like the old widow. It's like we have to "pin ourselves" to God with our prayers and not let go until God answers.

This is what prayer is. It is having a conversation with God!

- What prayers would you "pin" on the clothesline, now that you know it connects right to God? What things could you talk to God about?

Have older kids write some things down on index cards and literally pin them to the clothesline. Explain to all children that prayer doesn't always have to be things we want from God, but it can include treasures we learn when we study the Bible that we say back to Him! No matter what, God hears every prayer!

Craft: Prayer Bracelets

Materials

- Leather cording

- Purple, blue, brown, white, black and yellow

- Pipe cleaners (for younger children)

- Bead Prayer Color Reminder Chart

Instructions

Younger Children

Have younger children use pipe cleaners to string the beads to make a bracelet. Talk about how prayer is conversation to God, and how these beads will help us to remember the different things we can share with Him! Use the Bead Prayer Color Reminder Chart.

Older Children

Instead of pipe cleaner, use leather cording. String the beads, tie a tight knot to fit the student's wrist, and give them a copy of the Bead Prayer Color Reminder Chart to take home. Talk about the different ways we can pray.

As children are working on their prayer bracelets, talk about how praying is like sweet incense to God! (Psalm 141:2). When we find God's treasures in His Word and obey them, we can respond by offering those treasures back to Him in prayer.

Finished Product

Younger Children Version

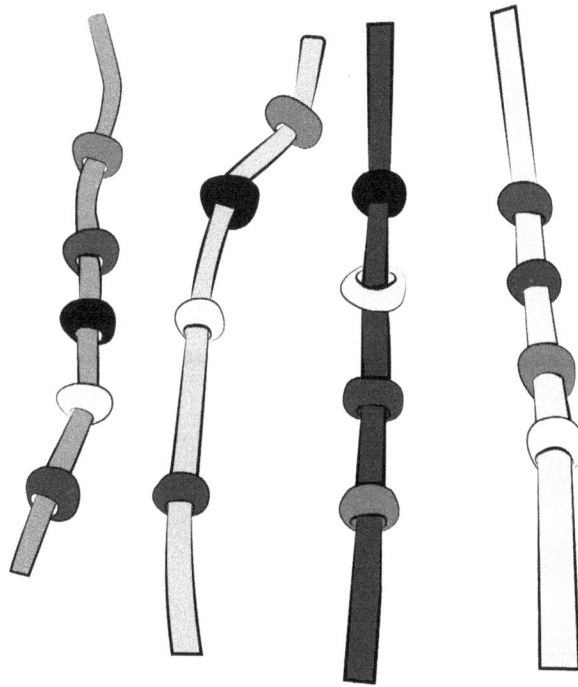

Older Children Version

Prayer Bracelet Bead – Meanings

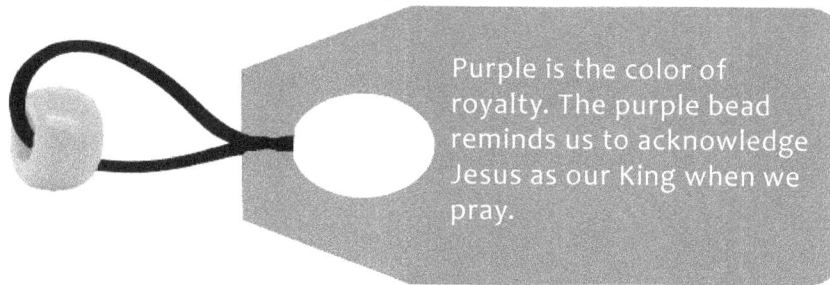

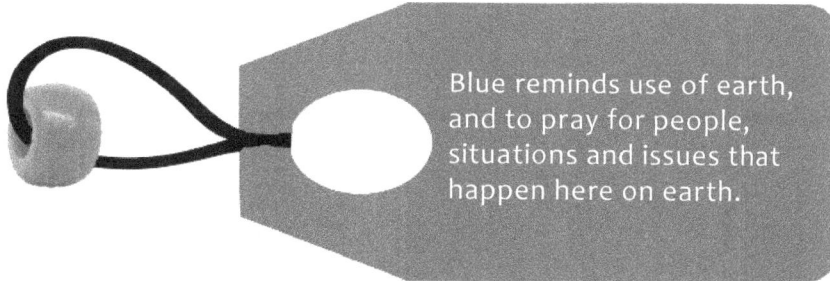

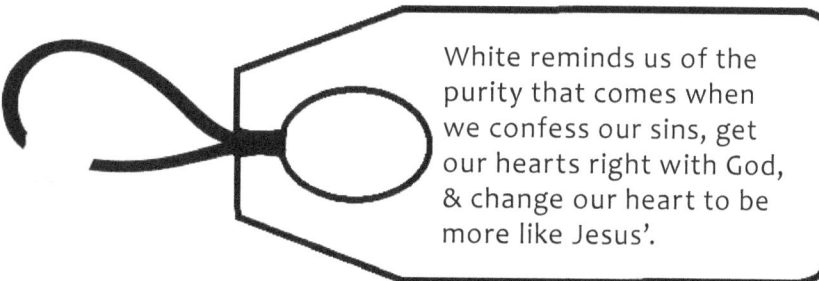

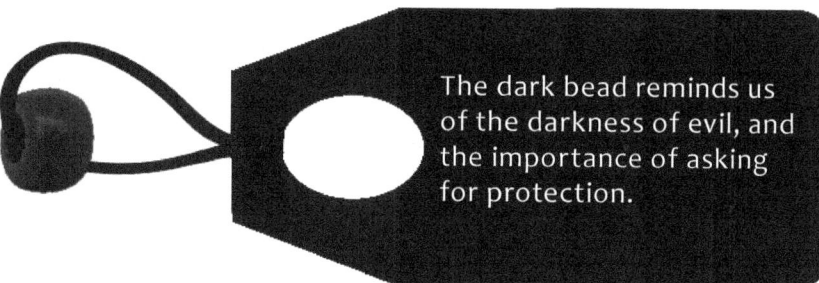

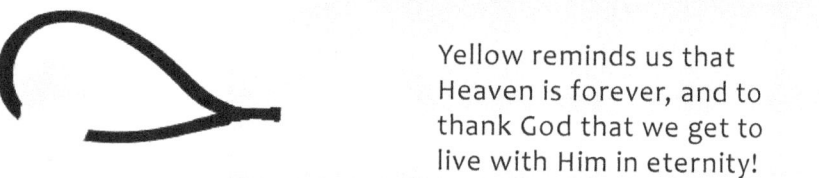

Purple is the color of royalty. The purple bead reminds us to acknowledge Jesus as our King when we pray.

Blue reminds use of earth, and to pray for people, situations and issues that happen here on earth.

Brown reminds us of bread. The brown bead reminds us to pray for daily provision—not wants, but needs for the day.

White reminds us of the purity that comes when we confess our sins, get our hearts right with God, & change our heart to be more like Jesus'.

The dark bead reminds us of the darkness of evil, and the importance of asking for protection.

Yellow reminds us that Heaven is forever, and to thank God that we get to live with Him in eternity!

ADDITIONAL RESOURCES

Inductive Bible Study App

Do you love the Inductive Bible Study method and wish you could do it wherever you go? Introducing the Inductive Bible Study App (InductiveBibleStudyApp.com). This one-of-a-kind app empowers individuals to grow in their faith by enabling them to study the Bible inductively using their favorite mobile or tablet device.

With this app, you can:

- **Mark Keywords** - Use images, and highlight, bold or italicize text (and more) for easy visual reference.

- **Take Notes** - Journal your personal study of the Scriptures and reflect on your growth.

- **Apply Themes** - Specify the theme of each chapter and even group verses together with division themes.

- **Perform Word Studies** - Understand the words of the Bible in their original language via the built-in Strong's concordance.

- **Research Cross-references** - Discover every instance that a word is used in the Bible to gain a comprehensive understanding of it.

Download the #1 Free Inductive Bible Study App today!

InductiveBibleStudyApp.com

Inductive Bible Study

Stop reading, start studying!

About the Author

Henry Jackson III, a bondservant of Jesus Christ. He is a native of Memphis, TN, who now calls Atlanta, GA his home. Henry primarily utilizes his spiritual gifts of teaching and leadership at Elizabeth Baptist Church in Atlanta, GA, where he currently serves as the Middle School Youth Pastor. Henry enjoys spending time with his darling wife Vanessa and son Henry IV, kayaking, racquetball, and mountain-bike riding.

Henry is the founder of Inductive Bible Study LLC, an organization that empowers individuals to grow in their faith by enabling them to study the Bible inductively using their favorite mobile device. Find out more at IndutiveBibleStudyApp.com.

As a Myasthenia Gravis (MG) survivor, Henry is a living testimony of God's healing power. Each day that God gives him the strength, he is constantly pursuing ways to glorify God and to make Him known to the world. A portion of the proceeds from the sale of this book will be donated to the Myasthenia Gravis Foundation of America, Inc. Find out more at www.myasthenia.org.